He is Here!

25 Days of Christmas Devotions

Browning Montgomery Wood

ISBN 978-1-68570-919-8 (paperback)
ISBN 978-1-68570-920-4 (digital)

Copyright © 2022 by Browning Montgomery Wood

All rights reserved. No part of this publication may be reproduced, distributed, or transmitted in any form or by any means, including photocopying, recording, or other electronic or mechanical methods without the prior written permission of the publisher. For permission requests, solicit the publisher via the address below.

Christian Faith Publishing
832 Park Avenue
Meadville, PA 16335
www.christianfaithpublishing.com

Printed in the United States of America

For His Name and His Renown!
(Isaiah 26:8)

For Braiden and Baylee Wood, my son
and my daughter. Live for the King.

CONTENTS

Introduction: Advent: 25 Days of
    Reflection vii
What Is Advent? ix

Day 1: What's in a Name? 1
Day 2: The Scandal of Nazareth 6
Day 3: This is Getting Weird!
          (Joseph's Dream) 11
Day 4: Who, Me? Why Me? (Mary's
          Favor) 17
Day 5: Wait! Did I Miss Something
          Here? 23
Day 6: Bring It On! 30
Day 7: Jump for Joy! 35
Day 8: History Will Tell! 40
Day 9: Oh, Little Town of Bethlehem ...44
Day 10: Sorry, We Don't Seem to
          Have Your Reservation 50

Day 11: "I Get No Respect!" 55
Day 12: Ponder On These Things 61
Day 13: "Remember? He Mentioned This Before!"...............................65
Day 14: A Different Kind of "Wise Guy" ...70
Day 15: Dear God…Not again! 75
Day 16: Welcome to Chisholm! 80
Day 17: The Three Hymns of Christmas....87
Day 18: "Wait! What Did He Just Say?" 92
Day 19: "He's Popping Up Everywhere!" ...97
Day 20: Who? Never Heard of Her…....103
Day 21: Timing is Everything!................109
Day 22: The Light of the World! 115
Day 23: Wonderful Counselor!...............121
Day 24: You Just Don't Get It, Do You?...126
Day 25: Be Born in Me! 132

Epilogue...139

INTRODUCTION

ADVENT: 25 DAYS OF REFLECTION

I want to invite you into a fresh look at Christmas and the twenty-five days of Advent. We will be looking at the scriptures we have heard all our lives, some with a fresh perspective, some with an old familiarity. There may be some of you who just haven't thought through it much and some insights that you may discover for the first time here in this book. I encourage you to read one Advent passage and reflection each day for the twenty-five days 'til Christmas. If you miss a day, that's okay; just pick up or double up on where you left off. Join me in the journey. Walk through Bethlehem with fresh eyes. Smell the hay where God rested. Hear the angels sing. Imagine the fear of common shepherds confronted with the angelic chorus. Consider with me, Mary, and what she must have been going through, along with Joseph as he sits dismayed that this is his reality. My prayer is that you never see aspects of the Christmas story the same way after reading this book. I can't promise you that you will, but I will try to offer you several new ideas that may make the holiness and intrusion of this event in human history that much more spectacular and awe-inspiring. *He is here!* The Advent of the Messiah has begun.

WHAT IS ADVENT?

The Advent is defined as the four weeks leading up to Christmas in which the Christian Church universally prepares for the arrival of the Messiah King spoken of throughout the ages in the prophecies of the Old Testament. It is in the dark winter solstice of December where the Light of the world is remembered. Its beginning as an annual celebration goes as far back as AD 380–400 and serves as an anchor for the end of the year, in the same way Easter and Lent capture our attention in the springtime each year.

The Latin *adventus* is the equivalent of the Greek *parousia*, meaning "the coming in human flesh," as well as meaning the Second Coming. This dual meaning is lost nowadays, but the idea is intact. Come celebrate the Advent of the Christ!

DAY 1

WHAT'S IN A NAME?

Scripture Passage

> The book of the genealogy of Jesus Christ, the son of David, the son of Abraham. (Matthew 1:1)

> And Jacob the father of Joseph the husband of Mary, of whom Jesus was born, who is called Christ. (Matthew 1:16)

Definition

Genealogy—noun. A record or account of the ancestry and descent of a person, family, or group.

Description

Many cultures keep precise records of descendants in order to trace the bloodlines and heritage of their people and/or its royal line.

Thought

Ancestry.com, 23andMe, and I'm sure many more are commonplace today. These are all genetic testing kits. You just swab the inside of your cheek, put it back in the box, mail it back to the company, and a lab processes your DNA from the sample to tell you where you came from, who else is in your family tree (some that you might not have been aware of), and to reveal the secrets of your family's history throughout the ages… as far back as they can identify! But why? What do we care? What does this information provide any of us? Maybe it is this; there is within the human soul a longing…a longing to know where we came from, a need to feel connected to our past and with those from our past. We use words like "heritage" and "ancestors" and phrases like "that's my people."

Matthew understood this all too well, he himself being a Jew and of Jewish heritage. Few people groups on earth have cherished, protected, and safeguarded their ancestral lineage like that of the Hebrews. But why? What's in a name? *Everything!* Especially for the Jew! Twelve tribes from twelve brothers, descendants of the great Patriarch Abraham, and especially for those of the Tribe of Judah, for it's been foretold by the prophets that the Messiah would come from his line! He (the Messiah) would become the Lion of the Tribe of Judah! So Matthew sets the tone from the very beginning of his Gospel by laying out the "23andMe" of Jesus. He points out the two greatest generational fathers, Abraham and David, but he doesn't stop there. Notice if you will, he includes some of the most unlikely characters, like adulterers, prostitutes, men obviously, but also women (not included in those days), heroes, failures, Hebrews, and Gentiles. It's not exactly the "who's who" of ancient Hebraic life, yet Matthew includes them all! Why? Well, of course, because it's the truth but also to help his readers understand this about the Messiah; this Jesus was from a diverse line, and sometimes a perverse line, but this baby that was to be born in a manger would save them all. Before the beginning of time, He was! His heritage is eternal, His DNA was supernatural! Before any of them were ever born, He existed and knew them. Before they were ever a part of his ancestral line, He existed.

Yes, for the Hebrew of that day, it would have added validation to his story and a historical record of His becoming the promised Messiah. Matthew lays it all out there when he ends verse 16 by calling Jesus "the *Christ*," the Greek word used for "Messiah." There are forty-two generations that Matthew lists with one simple point, *he's here*! "Listen Jewish brothers and sisters," Matthew says, "the greatest of our ancestral line has arrived! He's *here*! He's *really here*!" The Promise has come!

DAY 2

THE SCANDAL OF NAZARETH

Scripture Passage

Now the birth of Jesus Christ took place in this way. When his mother Mary had been betrothed to Joseph, before they came together she was found to be with child from the Holy Spirit. And her husband Joseph, being a just man and unwilling to put her to shame, resolved to divorce her quietly. (Matthew 1:18–19)

Definition

Pregnant—adj. having a child or young developing in a womb.

Description

At this point, Joseph and Mary were already "betrothed" or promised to be married to one another. In Hebrew culture, they were already considered husband and wife by contract even though they had not been wed or intimate with one another at this point. Mary had been at her cousin Elizabeth's for three months (Luke 1:36), and when she returns to Joseph, she is likely four months pregnant. Mind you, she is unmistakably pregnant!

Thought

You're what? What do you mean you're pregnant? Pause for a second…do you understand what has just happened to this young man? His worst nightmare has just been revealed to him. Have you stopped to consider how difficult this must have been for him to process? *Adultery, betrayal, shame, humiliation, defiance, stoning, death!* These are all words that describe this seemingly gentle passage of Scripture where we see the character revealed of the man who would be Jesus's earthly father. Make no mistake, all these words were in play!

The consequences of this reality were real! Mary most definitely would have been stoned to death by Jewish custom. Joseph would most certainly have been humiliated by the situation and would have been rightfully justified in seeing her displaced and stoned to death. Ahh…but this Son of David (v. 20) had been handpicked by God the Father in heaven to be "dad the father" on earth. He was no arrogant self-righteous man like many of his day. Notice, that even before the angel lets him in on a secret, that scripture tells us he was a "just" man (v. 19). He was "unwilling to put her to shame," instead he would divorce her quietly. This means there were likely those who probably encouraged him "to give her what she deserved!" "Have her stoned Joseph!" "She has humiliated you!" This might have been members of his very own family, yet Scripture says he was "unwilling" to put her to shame.

Can I ask you a question? How predisposed are you to cover an offense? How willing are you to love, in what seems like an unlovable circumstance? How quick are you to forgive a person and cover a betrayal that, if known, would shame the other person beyond social recovery? I remind you, these were steps Joseph took before the angel informed him on what was going on! He would prove to be even more righteous in the weeks and months to come as he would quietly bear the scandal of Nazareth, at the direction of an angel, for the love of his wife and the Savior of the World!

DAY 3

THIS IS GETTING WEIRD! (JOSEPH'S DREAM)

Scripture Passage

> But as he considered these things, behold, an angel of the Lord appeared to him in a dream, saying, "Joseph, son of David, do not fear to take Mary as your wife, for that which is conceived in her is from

the Holy Spirit. She will bear a son, and you shall call his name Jesus, for he will save his people from their sins." All this took place to fulfill what the Lord had spoken by the prophet: "Behold, the virgin shall conceive and bear a son, and they shall call his name Immanuel" (which means, God with us). When Joseph woke from sleep, he did as the angel of the Lord commanded him: he took his wife, but knew her not until she had given birth to a son. And he called his name Jesus. (Matthew 1:20–25)

Definition

Immanuel—noun. Defined as "God with us" (Isaiah 7:14)

Description

The circumstances haven't changed. Mary is still with child, and it is *not* Joseph's! He has some hard decisions to make, but his plans are about to be altered by *his* plans, the Lord God! The Lord of Hosts sends a messenger! Things are getting weird!

Thought

Have you ever had a dream? I mean a spiritual dream? One where you thought God "spoke" to you? Most people would say they haven't, but some, like myself, have.

Everyone I've talked to that has had a spiritual dream always mention the same question that I have had, "Was that God or just me having a strange dream?" That's a rational question, but it's not a question Joseph asked. Verses 20–23 of Matthew 1 are about his dream. He was still trying to decide what to do when God shows up! "Hey Joseph, I *am* behind all this! This is me! She is pregnant by the Holy Spirit's touch, and she is carrying the Salvation of the World!" "By the way…I want you to call him Jesus!"

Here is Browning's response two thousand years later, putting myself in Joe's shoes! It would go something like this: *"Huh?* Really? Let me get this straight, Lord? Mary, who I am betrothed to, is pregnant by the *Holy Spirit?* You say it's going to be a boy, that you want me to name Jesus or 'The Lord saves' and…he is the promised Messiah from Isaiah chapter 7—aka Immanuel—God with us! And I'm supposed to tell people this? Oh sure! This makes perfect sense! Who would doubt me? This is pure lunacy! I'm ruined…"

This is what blows me away…Joseph's obedience. There is no second guessing that we know of. There is no follow up questioning like "was that really of the Lord?" He just steps in and steps up! In the next remaining verse, he wakes up, marries her, and then remains celibate from her until Jesus is born. *Wow!* Utter obedience in the face of inevitable ridicule. This story is a *whopper*! This man is a wonder! His obedience is wild!

What if God asked this of you? Are you a person of wild obedience? If God has a whopper of a request for you, would you be ready to lay everything down and follow him? If there is one thing I have learned in my thirty-plus years of ministry, it's this— God will ask you to follow Him without question! He will ask you to step in or step up the way Joseph did. If you don't think He has yet, lean in and listen a little more closely.

You might discover He has been calling you to something amazing for a long time. May this Christmas be the advent of wild obedience in you! Dream! Believe! Act! Follow through in faith!

DAY 4

WHO, ME? WHY ME? (MARY'S FAVOR)

Scripture Passage

> In the sixth month the angel Gabriel was sent from God to a city of Galilee named Nazareth, to a virgin betrothed to a man whose name was Joseph, of the house of David. And the virgin's name was Mary. And he came to her and said,

"Greetings, O favored one, the Lord is with you!" But she was greatly troubled at the saying and tried to discern what sort of greeting this might be. And the angel said to her, "Do not be afraid, Mary, for you have found favor with God." (Luke 1:26–30)

Definition

Favor—noun/verb. approval, support, liking for someone or something; an act of kindness beyond what is due or expected.

Description

The Greek word used here is *charis* (car-is) meaning grace! We get our words charismatic and charisma from the Greek word *charis*. Mary has become the recipient of God's gracious gift!

Thought

When we consider the definition, along with the understanding of the Greek, we come to an interesting realization: God decided to *bless* Mary with carrying His Son! At first reading, we would jump to the conclusion that this passage is saying something different than it does. When it reads, "You have found favor," we could easily think Mary was of such righteous standing before God that He noticed her and picked her because of how pure or holy she was, but in truth, this isn't an acknowledgement of her being "holy" enough to bear the son of God, it's actually an enormous gift of grace that God is about to bestow on Mary. News flash! Mary was sinful just like you and me. Her deeds, actions, and behavior up to this point fell short of God's standard, just like you and me. There is nothing to indicate that she was of special stock such that God would choose her. No, this was an act of pure *grace* on God's part.

Stop! Because at first glance we could be thinking, *How is this a blessing?* She is going to tell a story no one will believe! She's going to be labeled as an adulteress for getting pregnant before getting married! She is going to be considered crazy as she shares the details of how all this happened! Mary would hardly feel like she was the recipient of God's grace, yet somehow she knows…she knows that it is indeed grace that of all the women, of all the world, in all of the history of the world before and after her, she alone will give birth to the Son of God. God the creator of the Universe, the maker of her very being, and her very womb is about to be bound up in her for nine months and enter the world as an infant.

She will nurse God at her breast—He who has always brought forth the bounty of the earth's supply (Psalm 145). She will clothe God—he who is robed in the stars and the sun (Psalm 104). She will change God's linens—He who has cleaned up after the sin and filth of mankind and his people for ages past (2 Chronicles 7:14). She will sing to God—the Lord who sings over us, the song of salvation (Zephaniah 3:17). Yes, indeed, grace has come to Mary…she is about to be the mother of God! Who can fathom what she must have gone through in trying to understand it? Who can possibly understand what she must have thought in the quiet moments of each day leading up to His arrival? Grace itself…who can understand it! Grace…the undeserved affection of God! That grace found Mary, and she'll never be the same because of it. I heard somewhere that grace is amazing…I agree.

DAY 5

WAIT! DID I MISS SOMETHING HERE?

Scripture Passage

> And behold, you will conceive in your womb and bear a son, and you shall call his name Jesus. He will be great and will be called the Son of the Most High. And the Lord God will give to him the throne of his father David, and he will

reign over the house of Jacob forever, and of his kingdom there will be no end. And Mary said to the angel, "How will this be, since I am a virgin?" And the angel answered her, "The Holy Spirit will come upon you, and the power of the Most High will overshadow you; therefore the child to be born will be called holy—the Son of God. And behold, your relative Elizabeth in her old age has also conceived a son, and this is the sixth month with her who was called barren. For nothing will be impossible with God." (Luke 1:31–37)

Definition

Virgin—noun/adj. a person who has never had sexual intercourse with another.

Description

Mary was quite young when she received this revelation from Gabriel, the messenger angel of God, but not so young to not know how conception works. She knew that babies came from the intimacy between a husband and a wife. She also knew she was a virgin, so what she just heard wasn't possible, but God was about to show her differently!

Thought

So what strikes me about this section of Scripture is what Mary draws from this conversation. She has just been informed that

a) she is going to give birth to the Son of the Most High.
b) He will rule on the throne of David!
c) He'll reign over the house of Jacob, forever!
d) oh yeah...and His Kingdom will have no end!

The Angel Gabriel has just told her that royalty, power, authority, title, and dominion were about to be born of her! She is a commoner. She is poor and without title or any kind of life yet. Mary's response was "Wait? Did I miss something here? Lord! I'm a virgin." And she was right! She knew enough to know about step one...there had to be step one in order to have a baby, and this was not a step she had taken yet.

The virgin birth is by far one of the most difficult aspects of the Christian story for many unbelievers to accept. It just sounds ludicrous. It flies in the face of science, but for believers, it is a hallmark of our faith, because it is by faith that we believe it. God says the same to Mary, "Mary, your own cousin, Elizabeth, is way too old to have a child, but you saw for yourself, she is six months pregnant! What makes you think I can't do the same in you? Nothing is impossible for me!" Wow! God just says it! "I can do anything!" And so He does!

Now look at the phrase from verse 35, "he shall be called holy." Have you ever wanted to know why the virgin birth was so important? Our sinful nature is passed on to us by two human parents. Adam and Eve bore sinful children, or better said, had children born in sin. Jesus though? Jesus is born of a woman, but also by supernatural means—the Holy Spirit who is *holy* and sinless. Jesus wasn't born of natural means to two human parents. Jesus was born of the supernatural. Jesus didn't inherit the death sentence of everyone born to two natural parents like you and me. Ephesians 2:1 says, "We were dead in our trespasses and sin." Jesus had to be born of supernatural means, otherwise He would have been born in sin like us and incapable of saving us! A sinner can't save other sinners.

Here is the crucial point! Because He (Jesus) was born of Mary, he was 100 percent human, and because He was born of the Spirit, he was 100 percent God. Both human and divine! The God/Man! God gave us the virgin birth so He could overcome sin and death by the supernatural power of His divine nature, and he was born of a woman so he could fully represent us in His human nature. The theological term used throughout history for this is *hypostatic union*. This is a huge theological point that I am simplifying greatly, but Mary would come to understand this in time, that her Son was not like any other boy born into this World. He is the God/Man…Immanuel… God with us! He is here!

DAY 6

BRING IT ON!

Scripture Passage

> And Mary said, "Behold, I am the servant of the Lord, let it be to me according to your word." And the Angel departed from her. (Luke 1:38)

Definition

Servant—noun. A person who performs duties for others, in particular those employed in a house or for domestic duties.

Description

The Greek word *doulos* (slave) is often used in Scriptural NT settings to emphasize total commitment. In English, we use the word slave and/or servant to compliment the idea of willing surrender to the authority of God in our lives. Mary declares herself as such in this verse.

Thought

Mary has just listened to the Angel Gabriel explain what is about to happen regarding her, and he points to the evidence that this is indeed possible, given that her elderly relative Elizabeth, barren and way beyond birthing years, is about to give birth to the great prophet John the Baptist in just three months. She, too, will be with child, and He will save the world, even though she is a virgin.

How would you have responded? Does something like "Wait, Lord, can we talk about this?" or "How am I supposed to explain this to my parents, much less to Joseph?" make more sense to you? Interestingly enough, neither of the responses are given, and I'm guessing we could imagine an additional half dozen or more really great follow up questions! Mary though…Mary doesn't do that at all. She says, "Bring it on!" No pause, no hesitation, not even a gentle cry is indicated… just a resounding, "Okay, I'm the Lord's servant, so let's do this!"

Part of me thinks this is just the teenager in her that was naive enough to not fully understand what she was getting into. The other part of me thinks, *and this is why God's grace rested with her.* Though grace is what God bestowed on her to bear His son, we have to understand she was a person that could do just that. She was a woman of titanium spirit! God didn't just spin a heavenly wheel or pull her lottery ticket and entrust the gift of grace to just anyone. No, God knew she was a willing servant! He knew she was up to the task! Mary was a "bring it on" spitfire. Remember the wedding at Cana? She called her son to action! She didn't shy away at the crucifixion either. She was right there watching her son take on the sin of the world. She witnessed His resurrected self and likely spoke some sense into Jesus's siblings as well. James, His half brother, became a key disciple and writer of the book of James. She was the right "servant" for the job.

How about you, are you a "bring it on" servant of God? Does He have your whole heart and undivided willingness to do what He asks of you? I hope so, because remember…He will ask you, He will call you, and you will have a decision to make! I hope it's "Bring it on!" We could use some more titanium spitfires these days!

DAY 7

JUMP FOR JOY!

Scripture Passage

In those days Mary arose and went with haste into the hill country, to a town in Judah, and she entered the house of Zechariah and greeted Elizabeth. And when Elizabeth heard the greeting of Mary, the baby leaped in her womb. And Elizabeth was filled with the Holy

Spirit, and she exclaimed with a loud cry, "Blessed are you among women, and blessed is the fruit of your womb! And why is this granted to me that the mother of my Lord should come to me? For behold, when the sound of your greeting came to my ears, the baby in my womb leaped for joy. (Luke 1:39–44)

Definition

Leaped—verb. to jump or spring to great heights or with great force.

Description

This is the first time the baby in Elizabeth's womb is in proximity to the child in Mary's womb. This unborn John the Baptist, who is to pave the way for the coming Messiah, is already making his first announcement by jumping for joy in Elizabeth's womb!

Thought

Do you understand the gravity of this event? I mean…do you really? *This is huge!* And I have seldom ever heard someone talk about it or even mention it. Needless to say, I absolutely *love* that Scripture records this moment! Why? Because God recognizes God in this moment, and He can't contain Himself! Look closer!

If you missed it, in verse 15 of Luke 1, the Scripture tells us that JB (John the

Baptist) will be filled with the Holy Spirit, even in the womb, before he is born. Wow! Now that's a new concept. This crazed, future Nazarite who will wear camel skin clothing, eat locust and honey, and live in the wilderness as a prophet of God was filled with the Holy Spirit before he was even born! (And some of you think your children have a weird outlook on life.) We also know this, Mary has had the Spirit of God hover over her (the Hebrew equivalent is Recaph, meaning to brood over, hover over). She is with child herself, and He is the Son of God!

So, what happens when the woman carrying the Son of God, approaches the woman carrying the Prophet of God, who is filled with the Holy Spirit of God? Answer: *Joy jumping*, that's what!

The third person of the Trinity can't contain Himself as the second person of the Trinity approaches! "Hey! Haha! You're here! Yes, I knew you'd come! Whooooo! I'm so excited to see you!" Cartwheels, front rolls, and abdominal herkies are the expression of the day in Elizabeth's womb! The Godhead is in present company with one another! Two out of the Three are gathered in the same place, with the third one looking on! And one thing we can understand from Scripture is that God is most happy and satisfied within Himself! The Triune God loves being with Himself. That is why this is so wonderful to understand! I love that God is excited to see Himself! Why? Because the unity of God as Father, Son, and Holy Spirit is vital to our faith. It is pivotal to our understanding of fellowship and essential to our wholeness in Christ. It may seem small to the casual reader, but for me, I jump for joy too! I jump for joy because God loves Himself and that brings me assurance of His love for me! Jump for joy this season, He is here! Immanuel, God with us! I hope you'll recognize Him in the way the Holy Spirit did on that day! And jump!

DAY 8

HISTORY WILL TELL!

Scripture Passage

> In those days a decree went out from Caesar Augustus that all the world should be registered. This was the first registration when Quirinius was governor of Syria. And all went to be registered, each to his own town. And Joseph also went up from Galilee, from the town

of Nazareth, to Judea, to the city of David, which is called Bethlehem, because he was of the house and lineage of David, to be registered with Mary, his betrothed, who was with child. (Luke 2:1–5)

Definition

Census—noun/verb. an official count or survey of a population, often providing important information.

Description

Common in the day was the idea of a census, a numbering if you will of the citizens, for the purpose of taxation and regulation. This is the first census taken while Quirinius is governor over Syria.

Thought

Leave it to the good doctor Luke to provide such detailed and traceable accounts of what took place the year of our Lord's birth. Most of us appreciate a timeline, and especially a historical timeline, that not only Scripture describes, but one that can be found in non-biblical texts as well. We have several verified historical names by Luke's account; Herod, Caesar Augustus, and Quirinius are all historical figures and serve as reference points in a historical timeline for the birth and life of Jesus in the New Testament. Rome kept extensive records. Josephus, the Jewish historian, and others add to the accuracy of these events happening.

Why should you or I care? We care because people trust historically accurate events over broad sweeping or inaccurate dating and timelines and certainly more than those things that are reduced to myths and legends. Luke wanted us to understand that what he was telling us is verifiable and real. History will tell that what he has recorded indeed took place, and the events leading up to the birth of Christ are factual. At first glance you may say, *well, whoopee…big deal*, but God wanted us to understand the timeline and the historical relevance behind Luke's account. Most certainly, there will be those who want to dismiss and discredit the account. Thanks, Dr. Luke, for setting the stage for this historical event. So glad that history will tell!

DAY 9

OH, LITTLE TOWN OF BETHLEHEM

Scripture Passage

> And Joseph also went up from Galilee, from the town of Nazareth, to Judea, to the city of David, which is called Bethlehem, because he was of the house and lineage of David, to be registered with Mary, his betrothed,

who was with child.
(Luke 2:4–5)

Definition

Bethlehem—noun. meaning "House of Bread." The traditionally held birthplace of the Christ child. Jesus later refers to himself as the Bread of Life.

Description

Bethlehem is currently located in the West Bank, a disputed area for Jews and Palestinians, resting just five or six miles south of Jerusalem. It's called "the City of David," the King's home and birthplace. Rachel died near it, and the Book of Ruth took place there. It was prophesied as the birthplace of the Messiah, according to Micah 5:2.

Thought

There is a history of Bethlehem often overlooked regarding an area near there, called the Migdal Eder. It is translated the "watchtower of the flock." The Old Testament prophet Micah tells us this in 4:8.

> As for you, tower of the flock, Hill of the daughter of Zion, to you it will come—Yes, the former dominion will come, the kingdom of the daughter of Jerusalem.

History tells us that Bethlehem and the surrounding countryside served a unique purpose in biblical times, as well as its flocks and its shepherds. This is where sacrificial lambs for the temple sacrifices were raised! Every year at the great Passover Festival of the

Jews and the various other festivals throughout the year, sacrificial lambs were needed, numbering in the hundreds of thousands. Special attention was given to these herds, and the ewes were protected and watched over with great care and preparation as they prepared to give birth to the lambs. When the lambs were born, they were inspected for blemishes or deformities of any kind. Their perfection and completely unblemished wool were of utmost importance. Lambs are known to thrash around after birth, so they would be swaddled, wrapped in cloth for warmth and protection, and placed in "mangers" until they settled down. I think I have heard a story like this? Is it sounding familiar to you, too?

These lambs were born for one purpose…sacrifice. To pay for the sins of those who they represented. Their blood was going to pay for sins, even the most unspeakable ones. It's said that the best and the largest majority of lambs sacrificed at Passover annually were from Migdal Eder…just outside Bethlehem. This is the ancient location of these herds (Genesis 35:21).

This child born in a manger and wrapped in swaddling clothes was not a mere infant and his being born in Bethlehem a mere coincidence, nor was it because of a census or just to fulfill the prophecy of Micah 4 and 5:2. God was going to help us understand just who this child would become! This child born near Migdal Eder was to become the final Lamb of God who would end the need for sacrifice forever. He would become the final sacrifice! His cousin, John the Baptist, would declare, "Behold the Lamb of God, who takes away the sins of the world" (John 1:29)! The shepherds would hardly have understood what they were gazing upon in that manger. The one…the last one…the final Lamb was born! He is here! It came upon a midnight clear. Redemption was born! This the Lamb of our Passover... Oh, little town of Bethlehem...did you even know?

DAY 10

SORRY, WE DON'T SEEM TO HAVE YOUR RESERVATION

Scripture Passage

> And she gave birth to her firstborn son and wrapped him in swaddling clothes and laid him in a manger, because there was no place for them in the inn. (Luke 2:7)

Definition

Inn—noun. an establishment providing accommodations, food, and drink, especially for travelers.

Description

The term *inn* has such a warm and inviting sense to it, doesn't it? A warm fireplace, a hearty meal, and a nice comfy bed bring pictures in our mind's eye. This would not be true for Joseph and Mary on this particular night.

Thought

You've been there, you have worked hard all day, maybe even driven for hours and hours to get to where you want to be.

All you want to do is get a room, take a nice hot shower or bath, eat a deeply satisfying Southern cooked meal, and slide between the sheets and sleep, oh how you want to sleep! Then you read the signs, "No vacancy!" "Full," "No Rooms Available," and your heart sinks and a deep sigh comes over you. *You have got to be kidding me! That's just great...* So you start calling. "Sorry, but we're all booked up." Oh no. This is getting bad! You didn't book ahead or pay a deposit fee to reserve a room, so you're stuck.

Then a farmer overhears your frustration and says, "Guess you didn't know the convention was in town?"

"No, I did not!" you reply.

"Well, it ain't much, but I have a heated barn. You're welcome to it if you'd like."

You agree with humble appreciation.

It's AD 3 or 4 in Bethlehem, your husband's hometown, and you're nine months pregnant and due anytime now. You have been riding a donkey all day, and you have just been informed the best available spot for you to rest and give birth is not in the inn as you'd hoped, but instead it is a barn, cave, or something like it. This night isn't shaping up as well as you'd hoped. *Lord, help me out here!* But it wasn't to be. This will be the humblest birth of a king ever!

But I can't help wondering…who took the last room in that inn? The room that could have been Mary's? Who took the last vacancy that bumped the birth of the Messiah into a barn? Would they have wanted to relinquish their room for her benefit? Maybe not, or maybe they did know and said, "Sorry, I'm too old to sleep on a floor" or "I would love to, but I have such a bad back!"

But here is a thought we can all consider…What has pushed the Lord out of the inn of your heart this season? What have you filled all the rooms with, so that He only gets the stable as His resting place? He deserves the presidential suite, but for many of us, even in this hectic season of Christmas, He has once again been resigned to the stable. He has been lost to the lights, the decorations, the frenzy of gifts, and the perfect Christmas dinner. How 'bout it, friend? Is there room in your heart's inn this season? Or will He hear "Sorry, we don't seem to have your reservation"? Let this King of King's be born in you again this season! *He is here!* Just open up!

DAY 11

"I GET NO RESPECT!"

Scripture Passage

> And in the same region there were shepherds out in the field, keeping watch over their flock by night. And an angel of the Lord appeared to them, and the glory of the Lord shone around them, and they were filled with great fear. And the angel said to them, "Fear not,

for behold, I bring you good news of great joy that will be for all the people. For unto you is born this day in the city of David a Savior, who is Christ the Lord. And they went with haste and found Mary and Joseph, and the baby lying in a manger. And when they saw it, they made known the saying that had been told them concerning this child. And all who heard it wondered at what the shepherds told them. But Mary treasured up all these things, pondering them in her heart. And the shepherds returned, glorifying and praising God for all they had heard and seen, as it had been told them. (Luke 2:8–20)

Definition

Shepherd—noun. one who tends to the care of livestock, such a sheep or cattle.

Description

Shepherds are probably one of the most well-known characters of the Christmas story, considered to be humble, simple folk who had the privilege of an angelic visit.

Thought

Cowboys! This term evokes a rough, tough, and rugged image in the minds of most people, as well as horseback riding, roping, and branding. There are images of cowboy hats, bandoliers, chaps, and campfires. Then there are shepherds…robes, sandals, staffs with a hook on the end. Shepherds, like Little Bo Peep, likes to wear robes. Side by side, there's little comparison! Little children don't play Shepherds and Indians! Westerns never portray the rough-and-tumble sheep herder, out for vengeance on those sheep-rustling scoundrels! No, sheep herders (aka shepherds) are seldom esteemed, recognized, or even acknowledged. This was never more true than in mid-ancient Israel. Even the first murder recorded in Scripture was of the shepherd Abel by his shepherd-hating brother Cain. Though many early Patriarchs were esteemed shepherds, others like the

Egyptians, hated them (Genesis 46:34)! Even King David was a noted shepherd. Yet they were considered lower working class, untrustworthy, or they were often the youngest in the family. Their testimonies were inadmissible in court. They were heaped in with tax collectors, prostitutes, the ignorant, and dung shovelers, but the Great Shepherd was coming to save the sheep of His pasture.

The God of Psalm 23 "The Lord is My Shepherd" was being announced and witnessed by the least likely sorts…shepherds. It was shepherds that would first see the Migdal Eder sacrificial lamb. It was shepherds, who couldn't testify in court, who would testify of the King who had come! It was shepherds that would see *the shepherd* of their salvation. This baby would forever represent them in a new and unforgettable way! They went from no respect to high praise! Turns out that the King of Kings, the Lord of Hosts, loves shepherds and is quite the shepherd Himself! So for every marginalized, forgotten, outcast, and overlooked person in society—*He is here*! Our Great Shepherd is here! He would later say, "My sheep hear my voice, I know them, and they follow me" (John 10:27)! I would say Jesus felt right at home, shepherding.

Baaah!

DAY 12

PONDER ON THESE THINGS

Scripture Passage

> But Mary treasured up all these things, pondering them in her heart. (Luke 2:19)

Definition

Ponder—verb. to consider something thoroughly and deeply, meditate upon.

Description

This type of reflection is not uncommon, most people have those introspective moments where they consider the magnitude of a situation or circumstance.

Thought

"Hey! Hey, are you listening to me?" It's that abrupt moment when you are caught up in a moment and someone hollers at you to "snap out of it!" It is in the quiet moments before we drift off to sleep and our thoughts race to a place we can't avoid. It's the moment you realize you're at your destination, but don't remember whether the lights you went through were red or green, yet you arrived just the same. We use phrases like, "I just need some time to think" or "I just need to clear my head." These are pondering moments. Some we seek, others we don't. Some we find… others find us. For Mary, they found her! Strangers (shepherds no less) show up right after a difficult and likely painful labor. They speak of marvelous encounters with angels, thousands of them, everywhere, all singing in unison and glorifying God! They mention "peace on earth" and "good will toward men," which must have been encouraging. It's all a little…overwhelming. She doesn't tell them thanks for stopping by or ask them follow up questions. She just…treasures these things. She treasures what's said and ponders it in her heart. "God this is real…isn't it?" "You just showed up to a group of shepherds and what they shared is amazing!" "I can't believe this is happening!" She is treasuring, pondering, putting the pieces together. She might have had this mind-blowing thought: *This really is the Son of God! I am the mother to the Savior of the world. How can this be?*

Ponder now for yourself. Go to the stable, place yourself there. Imagine all that has taken place, dreams, Elizabeth's house, Joseph's dream, seeing your abdomen slowly grow but knowing perfectly well you're a virgin, a journey to Bethlehem, prophecy, full inns, stables, mangers, shepherds, angels, heavenly choirs, peace on earth! What would you have treasured? What would your pondering have led you to consider? I sense a small smile on her sweet face as she looks down at her son. Can you see it too? She whispers, "Thank you, Jehovah, for choosing me, I love you."

DAY 13

"REMEMBER? HE MENTIONED THIS BEFORE!"

Scripture Passage

> All this took place to fulfill what the Lord had spoken by the prophet: Behold, the virgin shall conceive and bear a son, and they shall call his name Immanuel (which means, God with us). (Matthew 1:22–23)

Definition

Prophecy—noun. to say that a specific thing will happen in the future.

Description

Scripture is loaded with prophetic verses and passages, even entire books are solely prophetic. In fact, one-third of your Bible is prophecy! Did you know that? Over 33 percent of your Bible is prophecy. Do you think that means it's important? You bet!

Thought

None of us likes being left in the dark or left out of the loop! Most of us hate it when there is an inside joke, and we're on the outside of it. The phrase "Didn't you get the memo?" has become a cliché for intentionally being left out.

Guess what? That's not the Lord God! He knows He is mysterious enough as He is, so what does He do? Well, like any loving father, He gives us a heads-up! "Kids, gather 'round, in fact some of y'all grab a pen and write this stuff down. It's gonna be really important down the road." God has always been super generous with the prophetic. It's important to understand the gift of prophecy here. At its core, prophecy is about truth and those who tell the truth! Most of us mystify it and think of it as only telling the future, like a fortune-teller, or other unbiblical frauds, but you hear prophecy every Sunday from your pulpits, men and women who are the truth tellers of God's Word. There is, of course, the well-known truth tellers of future events, the Old and New Testament prophets. God uses these individuals to keep us informed and aware. Guess what? It is another act of God's grace to us as believers. God, in His infinite wisdom, knew we would keep asking questions, like petulant two-year-olds, and He, being patient and long-suffering, decided He would keep us in the loop. He did so we could recognize when things were happening just as He described. Why? Because it builds our trust, our belief, and our commitment to His plans.

Matthew understood this, so as each Old Testament prophetic event occurred, he reminded his Jewish readers that this was prophesied. "Look!" Matthew says. "This is exactly what He told us would happen!" Matthew shares no less than seven fulfilled prophecies between chapters 1:1–4:17. Hmmm, seven! The number of completeness in biblical numerology. How convenient! Not at all…God is a precisionist with exacting measure! And Matthew's gospel shouts with a spiritual megaphone! "Hey, chosen people of God, this is the One we've been waiting for! He is here! The undisputed heavy weight champion of the universe! The King of kings, the Lord of lords, the Messiah and Righteous One of God." Remember? He mentioned this before!

P.S. Jesus would go on to fulfill over three hundred prophecies of the Old Testament. The probability of one person fulfilling all these is determined to be so enormous that there isn't room to write it on this page. One study found that just forty-eight fulfilled prophecies is 1 to the 10157th power. That's 1+157 zeroes behind it, and that is just for forty-eight…of over three hundred!

DAY 14

A DIFFERENT KIND OF "WISE GUY"

Scripture Passage

Now after Jesus was born in Bethlehem of Judea in the days of Herod the king, behold, wise men from the East came to Jerusalem, saying, "Where is he who was born king of the Jews? For we saw his star when it rose and have

come to worship Him."
(Matthew 2:1–12)

Definition

Magi—noun. wise men known to be versed in astrology, mathematics, ancient literature, even magic.

Description

Thought to have arrived some two years after the birth of Christ, the Magi were likely priests of the Eastern regions of Persia and Babylon. Relics of Israel's former captivity (the days of Daniel) with knowledge of the Israelite prophecies are spoken of in Numbers 24:17.

Thought

Folklore holds that there were three wise men, based off the number of gifts that were given, that being three in number. In truth, we don't know how many came. Men of such renown would have traveled with quite the entourage! As gifted astrologers, they noted a star that was previously unidentified by them, a comet, supernova, major planetary alinement, maybe even an angel or a specified heavenly phenomenon special to Jesus's birth. No one really knows, but we do know this: long before the chosen people of God would seek to destroy this child's life (more than once as you'll see), these pagan wise men from a polytheistic region of the world identified the King of the Jews long before anyone else did.

They brought gifts worthy of His name and identity. But why? We aren't quite sure, but we notice a couple of things that are unusual.

First, they fell down and worshipped Him. I can't help but wonder here if these wise men were remnants of the influence of Daniel from his Babylonian and Persian captivity. Is it possible that Daniel was of such reputation and wisdom, along with the Shadrach, Meshach, and Abednego's of that age that they brought about monotheism and the worship of the one true God, even after so many centuries? Could their influence have had such a lasting impact? The wise men likely knew the Scriptures and the prophecies associated with this event.

Secondly, these supposed pagan wise men had dreams from God. They all had matching dreams from God…dreams that warned them to stay out of it and avoid Herod. This isn't the only incident where less than faithful men have had supernatural dreams, but it does lend itself to consideration.

Maybe these men were wiser guys than we know. They came to worship Him! Only gods were worshipped by these cultures. Who told them this infant, born in less than equitable surroundings, was God? Why would God give them dreams?

Granted, I am just speculating here! I admit that, but it does encourage me for my friends who are far from faith or distant from believing in virgin births, babes in mangers, eastern stars, and shepherds who see angel choirs. Maybe, just maybe…if Daniel had such a lasting impression and influence on these wise men, you and I can still leave lasting impressions on those we live out faith in front of every day. My prayer is that your witness and testimony will leave such a lasting impression that you too will be followed by wise men and women, who come to worship Him, lay gifts at His feet, and dream the dreams of God. Lean in! Have Daniel-like influence, show people by your life, and witness that the cliché saying, "Wise men still follow him," isn't cliché at all.

DAY 15

DEAR GOD... NOT AGAIN!

Scripture Passage

Now when they had departed, behold, an angel of the Lord appeared to Joseph in a dream and said, "Rise, take the child and his mother, and flee to Egypt, and remain there until I tell you, for Herod is about to search for the child, to destroy him." Then Herod, when he saw that he had been tricked by the wise men, became furious, and he sent and killed all the male children in Bethlehem and in all that region who were two years old or under, according to the time that he had ascertained from the wise men. (Matthew 2:13–18)

Definition

Infanticide—noun. the taking of innocent life, those of an infant or toddler.

Description

This passage of Scripture is not a beloved text of the Christmas season. It's obvious why, children are murdered in cold blood—a crime we call infanticide, likely the most hideous form of murder we can imagine. Yesterday, I told you the Jews tried to have Jesus eliminated more than once. This is the account of the wicked King Herod's genocide of the toddlers of Bethlehem.

Thought

Joseph has another dream and was so alarmed by the warning from God that they set out for Egypt in the dead of night, leaving nearly everything they owned but fortunately possessing the elaborate gifts of the Magi. 'Herod the Great' is livid that the Wise Men subverted him, so he decrees the death of every boy near the age of two years old in Bethlehem and the surrounding area. It was a massacre…thirty, maybe more, toddlers were slain. It would have been a modern-day horror story.

If you were paying attention in Sunday school all those years, you'll remember this event has happened before. It was 1,400 years earlier in the Book of Exodus. Exodus 1 records that the Hebrew people were large in number and under the rule of a Pharaoh who "knew not Joseph" (Exodus 1:8). The promise of a "deliverer" was known throughout the region, and the Pharaoh feared an uprising, so Pharaoh decreed that all male children were to be killed at birth, though many were saved by midwives. Pharaoh had the Hebrew infant boys collected and thrown into the Nile river to be drowned, food for crocodiles (Exodus 1:22). It was a massacre. But the deliverer of God's people would be spared…Moses was set out into the Nile in a basket sealed with pitch and rescued into the house of Pharaoh. He would rise to greatness and deliver God's people into the Promised Land.

Now again, in Matthew 2, infants are murdered because a deliverer has come! He will come out of Egypt again, as before, when Herod dies, fulfilling the prophecy told in Hosea 11:1: "Out of Egypt, I called my Son." He is the second and greater Moses, the true deliverer! A deliverer, now not just for the Hebrews, but for all of humankind. As before, this deliverer is spared, yet many lives are lost in an effort to see Him destroyed. But He does return from Egypt…and the world will never be the same because of it. He will finally lay down His life, so you can take yours up again! Jesus is the deliverer from sin and death! This child is the sin slayer and the death destroyer! Though these infants died and He was saved, this infant Jesus would die not many years later, for all to be saved! Thanks be to God!

DAY 16

WELCOME TO CHISHOLM!

Scripture Passage

But when Herod died, behold, an angel of the Lord appeared in a dream to Joseph in Egypt, saying, "Rise, take the child and his mother and go to the land of Israel, for those who sought the child's life are dead." And he rose and took the child and his mother and went to the land of Israel. But when he heard that Archelaus was reigning over Judea in place of his father Herod, he was afraid to go there, and being warned in a dream he withdrew to the district of Galilee. And he went and lived in a city called Nazareth, so that what was spoken by the prophets might be fulfilled, that he would be called a Nazarene. (Matthew 2:19–23)

Definition

Nazareth—noun. the small village in the lower Galilean hills between the Mediterranean Sea and the Sea of Galilee, thought to be inhabited by 200 to 1,600 people. It lies fifty-five miles north of Jerusalem.

Description

This was Joseph's hometown and the region where Mary lived as well. Jesus was foretold to be a Nazarene. Nazareth was a despised town, as was the region of Galilee, so a Nazarene from Galilee was doubly scorned and rejected in Jewish society. In John 1:46, the disciple Nathan says, "Can anything good come from Nazareth?" speaking of Jesus. It was the equivalent of being from an area of "undesirables" or equated with being "country bumpkins" in our day.

Thought

What part of town or your county does everyone look down on in your area? There is one area in every county or city that people make fun of and look down on. These areas conjure up images of ignorance, dirt track racing, and tacky Christmas light displays. The people are labeled as simple, poor, and even worse, "white-trash" and other sorts of offensive comments and racist implications. When I lived in Georgia, people made fun of people from Coosa; when in Florida, it was people from Bithlo. I am not from where I live now either, but I hear people tease about being from Chisholm. They say, "No wonder he is like that, he's from Chisholm" or "What can you expect from someone from Bithlo?" Even the names themselves have that ring of being despised…Coosa, Bithlo, Chisholm… at least by those who use them and see themselves as above them.

For the Jews, that was the town of Nazareth and anyone from the region of Galilee. People from these areas know how they are viewed, and some of them live into the stereotypes, and others rise above them and bring honor to their town. The arrogant and entitled avoid them, relishing in their own fortune above others misfortune. Such people are truly poor in spirt for judging these "others" in such ways. They have a "Bithlo" of the soul! But I find this interesting…

Nazarene looks and sounds almost identical to the Hebrew word "netser," meaning branch or sprout. The "branch" was a well-known term for the Messiah (see Isaiah 11:1). The Hebrew language at the time was written with only consonants, and "netser" would have appeared as NZR—the same main consonants as Nazareth. In Aramaic, the common language of the day, the word for "Nazareth" and the Hebrew word for "branch" sounded just alike. Muslims use the term Nasara (Nazarene) to describe Christians to this day. It is *not* a term of endearment. Christians were often called the Nazarites. The prophets said the Messiah would be despised and rejected (Psalm 22:6–7, Isaiah 53:3), so the reference to Jesus as a Nazarene was meant to reflect these passages. To be a Nazarene was to be despised and rejected, an outcast of society! Yet, this branch would become the vine of salvation.

We can imagine with the people of His day, such as Nathaniel, that judged where Jesus was from as an indication of the type of person He must be. "This can't be the Messiah, he's from Chisholm!" Labels, titles, the broken, the rejected, outcasts, and the abased, these are whom He loved, represented, and surrounded Himself with, not the religious, the entitled, the elite, or socially respectable. You know what I love about God? In everything He does, He displays humility and grace. Think about it, an obscure girl, from an obscure region, with an obscure husband, in an obscure village… mangers, shepherds, and then a town of not just no reputation, but one of disgraced reputation. The son of a carpenter would rise up to make Nazareth famous! This branch, this Nazarene would become the beacon of all who have felt discarded, left out, ignored, and rejected. He grew up poor and despised, yet he would become the representative and hero of all who have been treated like Him! I'm proud to be called a Nazarene, for as his followers, that is what we are! How about you?

Oh…and the sign into town. Well, it might now read: "Welcome to Chisholm (Nazareth)! Home of the King of kings, and Lord of lords!"

DAY 17

THE THREE HYMNS OF CHRISTMAS

Scripture Passages

And Mary said, "My soul magnifies the Lord"; Zechariah was filled with the Holy Spirit and Prophesied saying, "Blessed be the Lord God of Israel"; Simeon, he took him up in his arms and Blessed God and said, "Lord now

you are letting your servant depart in peace."
(Luke 1:46–55; 67–79; 2:29–32)

Definition

Hymn—noun. a religious song or poem of praise to God

Carol—noun. a song, especially of joy

Description

Mary, the mother of Jesus; Zechariah, the priest and father of John; and Simeon, a righteous man who comes to Jesus's circumcision, all break out in a song as they are recipients of the glory of God and His goodness.

Thought

What is your favorite Christmas carol? What hymn moves you more than any other this time of year? Is it like mine, the gentle and simple tune of "The First Noel"? Maybe it's the haunting minor notes and then the rising crescendos of "Oh Holy Night" as it calls us to fall on our knees, oh hear the angel voices, oh night divine, oh night when Christ was born! For believers, this season has always been a season of hymns and worship through carols. As long as I can remember, mom played those twelve-inch 33 1/3 rpm vinyl records on our turntable each season, ingraining the hymns and carols of Christmas into the hearts and minds of my sister and my brothers. The carols and hymns filled my imagination with images of wise men, mangers, and even little drummer boys! (I was so bummed when found out he wasn't really there.)

Here within the midst of the Christmas story, we find that so very common practice of faith in the three hymns of the Christmas story.

1. Mary would glorify God for having chosen her to be the most blessed woman in history.
2. Zechariah would bless the Lord for keeping His promise of a deliverer to Israel and that his son John would be His prophet to go before the Lord.
3. Simeon was told he would not die until He saw the Christ, the Lord's promised Messiah. (We will come back to him tomorrow)

These three give us Christmas hymns of praise to the Lord, and the carols have kept coming century after century, celebrating the birth of our Lord.

You may be like me, that each year you enjoy hearing the songs of the season, noting that they never grow old, sometimes because of the memories that come flooding in, and at other times, because you are reminded, like me, that this is a season of worship and reflection. "O' Come Let Us Adore Him," "Good Christian Men Rejoice!" "O Come All Ye Faithful!" "Joy to the World," and "Away in a Manger." God has come as an infant child to save the world, the hope of salvation has been born. So sing, friend, and join in singing the hymns and carols of Christmas, like those sung at the very first Christmas over two thousand years ago.

DAY 18

"WAIT! WHAT DID HE JUST SAY?"

Scripture Passages

> Lord, now you are letting your servant depart in peace, according to your word; for my eyes have seen your salvation that you have prepared in the presence of all peoples, a light for revelation to the

Gentiles, and for glory to
your people Israel. (Luke
2:29–32)

Definition

Gentile—noun. any person who is not of Jewish origin

Description

The common reference in the English text by Jews for people who are not Jewish is the term Gentiles, from the Latin *gentilis*, meaning "belonging to the same tribe or nation." In the Greek, *ethne*.

Thought

Here again, if you're not paying attention, you'd miss it. The casual reader would read through this short excerpt of Scripture and fail to notice the extremely controversial statement by the righteous and elderly man Simeon. You remember him from yesterday, and I told you we would come back to him. He is the third hymn writer in the three hymns of Christmas. But a closer look at what Simeon's hymn states would have brought its own version of shock and awe to his listeners!

"Wait! What did he just say?" Those within hearing distance and those who would have heard it repeated would have thought Simeon to be out of step and out of bounds with what he just said. Did you catch it? It's in verse 32, "a *light* of *revelation* to the *Gentiles*." Why would this have given the Jews pause, for it most certainly would have? Why, because he just said that the Gentiles would be blessed because of this infant. But…Simeon wasn't speaking of his own accord. He was filled with the Holy Spirit if you look at verse 27. He is speaking DUI (directly under the influence) of the Holy Spirit. His statement causes Mary and Joseph to "marvel" at what he has said (v. 33)! Yes! They marveled!

Jews had been disgusted by Gentiles for as long as Gentiles had been Gentiles and Jews had been Jews. The false gods of Gentiles and lack of conformity to the Law of God, as well as being the Jews' overlords more often than not throughout Jewish history, has caused a severe rejection of Gentile ways and Gentile people by practicing Jews. The promised Messiah was supposed to come and free the Jews from the rule of Gentiles, bringing judgement and swift wrath against Israel's oppressors. He would not be a friend to the Gentile and certainly not their salvation too…or so went the mindset of the Jew in that day.

Unless you're Simeon…and you're directly under the influence of the Holy Spirit. In the boldest of his statements while he is holding the Salvation of the Jews in his very arms, he says He'll be "a light of revelation to the Gentiles!" There it is, our hope clearly stated by Simeon! This Son of God is born for us "non-Jews" too! We are going to be included in the plan of Salvation. He is here! We are in!

God's sacrifice is broader than we dared dream, more inclusive than we dared imagine, more loving than we dared hope! Salvation just jumped the fence to come to a people that were told, "There's no hope for you." Jesus is born! The Gentile is saved! Thank God for Simeon's declaration! Merry Christmas, Gentiles! Salvation is born from the Jews!

DAY 19

"HE'S POPPING UP EVERYWHERE!"

Scripture Passages

Luke 1:15 (John); Luke 1:35 (Mary); Luke 1:41 (Elizabeth); Luke 1:67 (Zechariah); Luke 2:25 (Simeon); Luke 2:36–38 (Anna)

Definition

Holy Spirit—noun. the third person of the Trinitarian Godhead. The indwelling presence of God!

Description

The Holy Spirit is the third person of the Trinity, equal in every way to the Father and the Son. He is worthy of our worship, our attention, and our loyalty, the same as to the Father and the Son. He is the giver of spiritual gifts and the one who bears the Fruit of the Spirit within us.

Thought:

Right out of the gate in Luke's Gospel, repeatedly we are introduced to the third person of the Trinity, the Holy Spirit, like never before in Scripture! The Old Testament makes passing mention of Him from Genesis 1:2 until the final Old Testament prophet of God in Malachi 2:15. We may have thought of Him as more of a superpower in the Old Testament accounts of His role in the lives of Samson, the mighty, and David, when he defeated Goliath. We certainly understand the prophets spoke by His leading (see 2 Peter 1:21), but something new is happening here at the birth of the Messiah, something God has not done before…common people are being filled with the Spirit in large numbers. As you read Luke, don't miss the continual references to the Holy Spirit. He's popping up everywhere! Mary, Elizabeth, her husband, and John, who is still in her womb, doing cartwheels by the infilling of the Holy Spirit. Simeon and Anna, two more unknowns, make it into the Luke narrative and prophesy by the Spirit's leading. *Why…* this isn't about Him, it's about Jesus and the birth of the Savior of the world, isn't it? Maybe, but this is about Immanuel "God with us", in a whole new way!

Holy Spirit will descend on Jesus like a dove at His baptism and fill the Lord with His presence (Matthew 3:16, Mark 1:10,

Luke 3:22, John 1:32–33) and remain on Him! The Holy Spirit is here, and now in full view of the onlookers at Jesus's baptism. His cousin John declares to the crowd that is gathered there that he has been baptizing them with water, but Jesus will baptize them "with fire and the Holy Spirit." I want to suggest something to you, and here it is. Immanuel "God with us" was about to become permanent and pervasive. You cannot read John 14, 15, and 16 and miss it! These three chapters are Jesus's dissertation on the Holy Spirit! He spends three chapters talking about the Holy Spirit's coming and the need for Himself to "go away," as He puts it. Why? Because "God with us" is about to take on a whole new meaning!

Every denomination and creed of the faith recognizes this fact. At salvation, there is transformation! The out-filling of the dead human spirit, with the in-filling of the Spirit of God! The Baptism of the Spirit follows as we open our hearts to receive it! Now Immanuel (God with us) is everywhere, in every believer! Jesus, who was one man, has now filled every man and woman who believes. He is in us all, all over the world, God as the Holy Spirit! The ultimate expression of "God with us"! Millions upon millions filled with love, joy, peace, patience, kindness, goodness, gentleness, faithfulness, and self-control…forever altering the landscape of the world.

Yes, it starts with a handful of commoners in Luke's Christmas narrative, but soon the commoners will become the culmination of the full-time representatives of Immanuel…God with us! The glory of Christ in the world, in the hearts of His followers! Yes, the Savior has come, and He has brought a gift to us with Him. Unwrap the Holy Spirit this season and be "God with us" to the world around you! He is here!

"Now we have not received the spirit of the world, but the Spirit who is from God, so that we may know the things freely given to us by God" (1 Corinthians 2:12).

"Do you not know that you are the Temple of God and that the Spirit of God dwells within you?" (1 Corinthians 3:16). *Immanuel!*

DAY 20

WHO? NEVER HEARD OF HER...

Scripture Passage

And there was a prophetess, Anna, the daughter of Phanuel, of the tribe of Asher. She was advanced in years, having lived with her husband seven years from when she was a virgin, and then as a widow until she was eighty-four. She did not depart from the temple, worshiping with fasting and prayer night and day. And coming up at that very hour she began to give thanks to God and to speak of him to all who were waiting for the redemption of Jerusalem. (Luke 2:36–38)

Definition

Fasting—verb. voluntarily not eating or abstaining from something for a period of time.

Praying—verb. an act of requesting help or expressing of thanks to God.

Description

The prophetess Anna was a well-known figure around the Temple in her day. She was dedicated to fasting and praying there. You may not have ever heard of her. She says, "Nice to meet you!"

Thought

If you're like me, you never really noticed Anna. Having read Scripture for decades, including the Christmas story, birth of Christ narratives, I've never really taken time to look at these three simple verses from Luke's Gospel. When we do, we learn a lot in a very short time! We learn she is a notable prophetess, a daughter of a less than notable man named Phanuel, of the less than notable tribe of Asher (eighth son of Jacob and a tribe of no real merit—no heroes or judges). We find out she's a widow, married a mere seven years, and now she's old at eighty-four. But verses 37 and 38 tell us why she is mentioned and why her name is etched into the Gospel of Luke and the cannon of Scripture for all of time! *She was a warrior!* Luke says she prayed, fasted, and worshipped day and night at the Temple. No wonder she was a prophetess!

As a result of her faith and persistence to honor God, deny herself, pray, and worship God all these years, she was able to lay her eyes on the promised "redemption of Jerusalem" and testify to His arrival. Notice it in verse 38! God blesses her prayers, fasting, and worship by revealing His Son to her right there along with Simeon. For most people, if I mentioned this woman of God, they'd say, "Who? Never heard of her…" But God knew her, and she knew God. Their relationship was such that He saw fit to bless her socks off and use her to proclaim the coming of the Messiah as the "redemption of Jerusalem."

Let me ask you a simple question. What have you given up on? What have you stopped praying about, stopped believing God for? I want to encourage you today to go "Anna" on that issue! Like Anna who never gave up on seeing the redemption of Jerusalem, start praying again, fast again, or do both for the first time ever! *Press in!* Press in for what you want to ask of God this season or for the new year. Day and night worship, pray, petition, and let your request be made known to God (Philippians 4:6)! He says if we draw near to Him, He will what? That's right! He will draw near to *us*!

We can safely assume this was an eighty-four-year journey for Anna. Since she was a little girl, she'd heard the rumors, the stories, the Scriptures that told of His coming, and now after all this time… He is here! You, too, may feel less than notable, from a less than notable family, with a less than known history or fame, but it would seem that's whom

God is listening to, and whom He rewards as we earnestly seek Him! So press in brother, press in sister, He is not slow in keeping His promises (2 Peter 3:9)!

DAY 21

TIMING IS EVERYTHING!

Scripture Passages

> But when the fullness of time had come, God sent forth his Son, born of woman, born under the law, to redeem those who were under the law, so that we might receive adoption as sons. And because you are sons, God has sent the

Spirit of his Son into our hearts, crying, "Abba! Father!" So you are no longer a slave, but a son, and if a son, then an heir through God. (Galatians 4:4–7)

Definition

Timing—noun. the choice, judgement, or control of when something should be done!

Description

"Timing is everything," someone said. Have you ever wondered why all this went down the way it did? Why did it happen when it did? Galatians isn't usually where we turn for Christmas passages to share with the family, but today we will, for it truly belongs there.

Thought

Notice the opening phrase, "When the fullness of time had come, God sent forth his Son." We might say it like this, "When everything that needed to happen, happened… and at the best time possible, God sent His Son." You have probably asked, just like me, "Why then Lord?" If you wanted to get the message of salvation out, now would have been the best time! Jesus could be on TBN, CBN, and disrupt ABC, NBC, CBS, CNN, and FOX with His miraculous healings and raising others from the dead. He would have social media coverage and followers like no one else! Facebook, Rumble, Snap, TikTok, Instagram, Telegram, Twitter, Fitter, and

Fodder! Imagine His tweets! "Walked on water today, Peter not so much!" Jesus would be everywhere! Millions of followers and the same number of haters, but His reach would be unparalleled in human history. God, was your timing off? Not at all!

We need to remember for whom He came, the Jews. The promise was to them. Put aside your Western, North American Christianity for a day. Jesus was Jewish and came for them first (Romans 1:16). Let's set the stage. There has been four hundred years of silence by God…no prophecies, some wars, but the silence was deafening. During this period, the Law had grown in the hearts of the Jews to a point of choking restriction; the arrogant few, who strove to keep it perfectly, judged all who didn't. The Jews were under the yoke of oppression by the heathen, polytheistic, and very sadistic Romans. The Romans had learned the most devious and atrocious form of capital punishment known to man—crucifixion—and they used it liberally on the Jews, for whom it was a curse to be killed in this way (Deuteronomy 21:22–23). Enter Jesus…He would defy the imagination of every Jew He encountered. The evidence for Him being the promised Messiah was mounting daily, as prophecies were being fulfilled. His healing power exceeded anyone before Him, and as such was the unmistakable mark of the Chosen One. He was teaching on the law with authority and in a way no one had ever heard of. He was keeping it perfectly to the true letter of the law, correcting those in authority who had suffocated the Jew under it, and warping it for their own gain.

Now He would face down the Roman Empire, he would bear the shame, the humiliation, and the curse of their demonic torture instrument—the cross. He had to die the worst death imaginable in human history, and He had to die in complete innocence, according to the prophecies spoken hundreds, even thousands of years, before He arrived.

Yes, timing is everything! God knew that after these four hundred years of silence, He was about to speak again and never stop speaking thereafter through Jesus, Scripture, and the Holy Spirit! He knew the timing was perfect for the prophecies to be fulfilled through the virgin and her son, the salvation of the Jews. God knew that to pay the price for the sin of mankind, His Son must undergo the most treacherous death imaginable, and so He would…willingly. The King born to die! Immanuel, God with us! Thank you, God, for your perfect timing! We await your magnificent *return*! And we trust your timing in that as well! We will shout again! He is *here*!

DAY 22

THE LIGHT OF THE WORLD!

Scripture Passages

The people who walked in darkness have seen a great light; those who dwelt in a land of deep darkness, on them has light shone. (Isaiah 9:1–2)

I will give you as a covenant for the people,

a light for the nations. (Isaiah 42:6)

I will make you as a light for the nations, that my salvation may reach to the end of the earth. (Isaiah 49:6)

And leaving Nazareth he went and lived in Capernaum by the sea, in the territory of Zebulun and Naphtali, so that what was spoken by the prophet Isaiah might be fulfilled: "The land of Zebulun and the land of Naphtali, the way of the sea, beyond the Jordan, Galilee of the Gentiles— the people dwelling in darkness have seen a great light, and for those dwelling in the region and shadow of death, on them a light has dawned. (Matthew 4:13–16)

Definition

Light—noun/verb/adj. Light or visible light is electromagnetic radiation within the portion of the electromagnetic spectrum that can be perceived by the human eye.

Description

Do you know how "darkness" is defined? It is "the partial or total absence of light," so technically speaking, there is no such thing as darkness, there is only the absence of light.

This absence of light leaves us in what we call…darkness.

Thought

Have you considered how dependent we are on light? The human eye is incapable of seeing anything without it! The ability to see color is dependent on light. Light reveals everything to us. I went caving (spelunking) one time with a group, into utter darkness. We went deep into the earth, turned off all our headlamps and flashlights, and I shared a short lesson. It was pitch black down there. It was impossible to see, and I was wearing a watch that illuminated in indigo blue. I said "watch" this (no pun intended)! The light from that small wristwatch illuminated the whole cavern space we were in! We easily recognized one another, and we all focused on the light from the watch. Though it was very small, the light pierced the darkness!

Jesus, of course, would go on to fulfill the Isaiah prophecy from chapters 42 and 49 by moving to Galilee according to Matthew 4. Light is everywhere in this story of the birth of Christ! The light of the star, Gabriel always appears as a great light; the shepherds see the light of the heavenly host as they sang on high! Both Zechariah and Anna speak of the coming light to the nations and the Gentiles. The truth is light is essential for life! We need the light! In its absence, we search for it; in the night sky, we marvel at it; in the summer, we bask in it. The seasons are revealed and change with it. There is no reading without it. There is no movement by man or beast without it. There is no air to breath without it (photosynthesis). Light brings warmth and can be focused into a narrow beam as a laser. Light heals, and light reveals!

Jesus Himself would say it outright in John 8:12, "I am the Light of the World. Whoever follows me will not walk in darkness but will have the light of life." He became the light to the Jews, who would believe, and even more so to us, the Gentiles, who would believe as well. I wonder this season, have you seen the Light? Does your soul live in the darkness of this world? Are you wandering around blindly in this world without the Savior? Let me tell you, brother or sister, you cannot see without the light giver! Your blindness will not be lifted until you invite the Light (Jesus) to illuminate your heart to faith! Jesus is the light of the world! May His light be lit in you! This little light of mine, I'm gonna…! Enough of the darkness! Shine the Light of salvation!

DAY 23

WONDERFUL COUNSELOR!

Scripture Passages

> For to us a child is born, to us a son is given; and the government shall be upon his shoulders, and his name shall be called Wonderful Counselor, Mighty God, Everlasting Father, Prince of Peace. (Isaiah 9:6)

Definition:

Counsel—noun. advice; opinion or instruction given in directing the judgment or conduct of another.

Description:

A counselor, a person who gives said advice and instruction for directing good judgement or conduct. There are those for whom this is their profession, but long before this was a professional occupation, Jesus was named the Wonderful Counselor.

Thought:

Today's passage is a famous Old Testament passage from the prophet Isaiah. Here, the prophet says Jesus will be the "wonderful Counselor," but what does this mean for you and me? "Wonderful Counselor" in Hebrew is *pele-yoez*. Pele means "a miracle, a marvel, a wonder," indicating "something extraordinary, incomprehensible, inexplicable." The second term (yoez) means "to advise, counsel, devise, purpose."

Before he conquered death and sin, Scripture tells us in two separate places why He is our wonderful counselor. Hebrews 4:15 says, "For we do not have a high priest who is unable to sympathize with our weaknesses, but one who in every respect has been tempted as we are, yet without sin." Then the shortest verse in the Bible reads, "Jesus wept" (John 11:35). We've already talked about how Jesus was 100 percent God and 100 percent man at all times while on earth as the God/Man. I think sometimes it's the man part we diminish. Yet, these two verses do us a huge service! The first in Hebrews tells us He sympathizes with us and our weaknesses.

The second verse in John shows us He indeed does sympathize with us. Jesus weeps at the loss of his friend, Lazarus, and with His sweet friends, Mary and Martha, Lazarus's sisters. They all loved Lazarus so much. The Jews even say, "Look how much He loved him." Here what's so amazing—Jesus already knew he was about to raise Lazarus from the dead, so why weep? I can hardly imagine myself being upset when I know I'm going to see my friend again in about five minutes with a simple command of "Come out!" Yet, I am not the wonderful Counselor, am I? I don't understand the full depth of His humanity, do I? I don't comprehend Him as having the greatest compassion, the deepest love, and the most in touch emotions of any human who ever lived, yet He did! For that is the nature of God, the best of every human emotion and feeling. Scripture constantly affirms that Jesus was "moved with compassion."

Guess what, dear friend in Christ, He still is! He sees our deepest hurts, our most damning shame, and our most overwhelming losses. The death of our loved one at this time of year is His hurt too. The stress of our loved one in the hospital is His stress too. The feeling of loneliness and aloneness is His feeling, too. He is still moved with compassion! That is why we pray, because it is here in prayer that He comes…and He always comes and lays His hand on our shoulder or wraps us up in peace that surpasses understanding. He whispers, "I'm here." He whispers, "I love you." He cannot escape His human emotion and compassion for you, for this is His spiritual nature first! He is our Wonderful Counselor, our Prince of Peace! Pray today and listen to the Wonderful Counselor speak over you. Christmas is hard for many people. Thankfully, we have a wonderful counselor who understands the "hard." Thankfully, He is here! Amen.

DAY 24

YOU JUST DON'T GET IT, DO YOU?

Scripture Passage

When Herod the king heard this, he was troubled, and all Jerusalem with him; and assembling all the chief priests and scribes of the people, he inquired of them where the Christ was to be born. They told him, "In Bethlehem of Judea, for so it is written by the prophet: 'And you, O Bethlehem, in the land of Judah, are by no means least among the rulers of Judah; for from you shall come a ruler who will shepherd my people Israel.'" (Matthew 2: 3–6)

Definition

Chief priests—noun. principle men of the priesthood, both active and deposed, often heads of twenty-four priestly divisions. Scribes were the experts of the Law and Scripture.

Description

These were supposedly the most noted authorities on the Old Testament texts and prophecies. They were the experts of their day.

Thought

Do you know a person, that regardless of what you say or the evidence you show them, they still just don't get it? We say things like, "I explained it until I was blue in the face!" or "It was like talking to a brick wall!"

Enter the chief priests and the scribes of Herod's court. Herod, unknowledgeable in the Scriptures, asks his scribes and chief priests to tell him where this savior or ruler is supposed to be born, based on what the wise men have just told him! Guess what? They knew the answer! They immediately shared the prophetic scripture from Micah 5:2 as the promise of where the ruler would be born! Then Scripture tells us as soon as Herod stormed off, they immediately went back to their rooms and packed up their things and made haste to catch up with the wise men's caravan to Bethlehem, so they, too, could witness the birth of the savior and fulfillment of Micah 5:2! Right? Wrong! They did nothing…absolutely nothing.

Wise men, extravagant caravans, unexplainable stars, and celestial phenomena, rumors of the coming Messiah circulating, and now evidence that it's possible He has arrived! What does a sane person do, a chief priest or scribe, a resident authority on all things God and prophetic? They say good night and head off to bed. Really? That's it! These professors, these heads of academia, these respected sages, and authorities on the Law just go about their business and back to the status quo. I want to scream, "You just don't get it, do you?" And sadly, they didn't.

Truth is…not much has changed. This story is told year after year, Christmas season after Christmas season, and people stand on Christmas Eve night with loved ones and close friends, candle in hand, carols in voice, heads bowed in prayer. Sadly, it's someone else's prayer, and the song is just a sentimental expression of the season. The candle just makes for a pretty scene when we all raise them at once.

It's regretful that in every sanctuary, all around the world, there are still scribes and chief priests sitting in the room. They've read, yet they don't understand. They've heard, but they've never listened. They've even spoken, but don't truly comprehend. They just don't get it. They go through the motions of Christmas, but never encounter the Christ of Christmas.

You are one of two people reading this today. A genuine Christ follower, committed to His mission and His ministry to this broken world, or you are a follower of Christmas traditions and next week, it will be status quo for you again. I wonder…do you get it? Will another season come and go and your heart with it? Wise man or woman…or scribe? The savior is born! Rush to worship at His side. Don't sit idle again another year! Come and worship the Savior of the world!

DAY 25

BE BORN IN ME!

Scripture Passages

> For God did not send his Son into the world to condemn the world, but in order that the world might be saved through him (John 3:17).

Definition

Born—adj./verb. existing as a result of birth.

Description

The moment has arrived, the culmination of countless ages, hopes set on the promise of a Messiah. Prophets, angels, and dreams have come to a pivotal moment in history. After this night, all of human history and the calendar we follow will be divided in two, BC and AD—all because a baby was born.

Thought

Mary has reached full-term with the child in her womb. There is no stopping it now. The child must and will be born of her. In the quiet of the night, his cry is heard, he sleeps and nurses at the breast of his human mother. He is helpless…think about that… God is helpless…for the first time since there was time. The infinite has entered the finite.

The timeless God has entered time with mankind. He will rely on His mother and His earthly father to care for Him, as he grows to become the man who would forever change the world. Everything I have shared with you in the past twenty-four days would be for nothing if you miss this…Jesus is the Son of God, and He has indeed forever changed the world, coming to bring life to those who'd believe! Indeed, He is *here*!

Let me ask you, friend. Has Jesus ever been born in you? John 3:17 written above tells us He didn't come to condemn you and judge you, rather He came to *save* you from judgement and condemnation, which we rightly deserve. Scripture tells us that we are spiritually dead because of our sin and trespasses (Ephesians 2:1). Jesus said e came to give us life and give it to us abundantly (John 10:10)! He told Nicodemus all he had to do was be *born* again (John 3:3). There is a human birth, which we have all experienced, but greater still is the spiritual birth! Only the Spirit of God can bring our spirit back to life; this is what Jesus meant when He said you must be born again.

The book of Romans walks us through understanding how we are born again.

First, we have to understand that we have indeed sinned, and offended God by doing so. Romans 3:23 reads, "For everyone has sinned and fallen short of the glory of God."

Second, we have to understand sin has marked us for death. Romans 6:23 says, "The wages (price) of sin is death." That is eternal separation from God.

Third, we cannot save ourselves, because we are sinful. Romans 5:8 says, "God demonstrated His love for us in this way, even though we were sinners, Christ died for us." The price was paid in full by God, through Jesus.

Forth, we must believe and receive! Romans 10:9–10 declares, "If you confess with your mouth Jesus is Lord, and believe in your heart God has raised Him from the dead, you will be saved; for with the heart one believes and is made right with God, and with the mouth He confesses and is saved." We believe in faith that Jesus is Lord, and with our mouth we tell the world the same! That is being born again!

I wonder, have you ever committed your life to following the Lord Jesus? Jesus calls it being born again, or Him being born in you. Let this Christmas Day, or whichever day you read this, be the day He is born in you. Become His new manger of rest, his Bethlehem, his Nazareth, His home.

Here is a simple way to do that, it's as simple as A, B, C, and D.

Admit—Admit you have sinned against Him, tell Him you realize that, and ask His forgiveness.

Believe—Believe that he has died for you, in your place. Trust Him to guide your life and invite him to be Lord of your life.

Confess—We confess with our mouths, telling others of your decision to follow Him. Declare "I'm a believer," "I'm a Jesus follower." It's a public declaration of your decision.

Determine—Determine to live your life under His direction and leadership. We call this being a "disciple" (Romans 12:1–2). Now our lives reflect His own in as many ways as possible.

You can pray this prayer as a prayer of commitment to the Lord.

> Lord God, I believe Jesus is in fact the Christ, the Savior of the world. I believe he was born, lived a sinless life, and then was crucified for me. I am a

sinner. I need your forgiveness. Please forgive me, and I receive Jesus as my salvation. I wish to be born again! Jesus, I receive the life you have promised to those who would believe in you. And I will follow you with the rest of my life as my Lord and Savior. Thank you for saving me! I love you! In your name, Jesus. Amen!

Guess what? He has been born in you if you just said that simple prayer with a genuine heart! Welcome to the family of God. He is here with you always!

EPILOGUE

IT'S CHRISTMAS! HE IS HERE!

My prayer all along for you as you read this book is that you would discover something new, learn something important, be filled with awe again for Christmas, and maybe even realize he came to be your savior just as much as for those like me that already believe.

There is one important step left…discipleship. Just like how the infant Jesus needed loving care and nurturing in order to grow into the man of salvation he would become, new believers need to be nurtured and grown in the context of other faithful believers who can guide and instruct them. Seek out a church that is seeking after Jesus and one that believes in the power of the Holy Spirit. That is the beginning of discipleship. I will help in as many ways as I can, but also seek out growth opportunities at your end. We have prayed over each of these books that the Lord would anoint them with the blessing of the message of Jesus. Be sure to pass it on to others who need to know.

He is here!

ABOUT THE AUTHOR

Browning is originally from Lubbock, Texas. He has served in churches in Texas and throughout the Southeast. He is currently serving in his thirty-fifth year of ministry with a world missions organization committed to church planting and discipleship in East Africa.

Learn more about Browning's ministry, email him, and leave comments. Learn how you can support the ministry and give online at www.barrywoodministries.org—a ministry dedicated to evangelism, discipleship, and church planting in East African countries and beyond. The ministry is also working to provide clean water, AIDS education and awareness, medical relief, and more. Join us in reaching the world for Christ until all can say, "He is here."

www.ingramcontent.com/pod-product-compliance
Lightning Source LLC
Chambersburg PA
CBHW021014121125
35345CB00020B/52